Boost
Brainpower

by
Varinder Aggarwal

V&S PUBLISHERS

Published by:

V&S PUBLISHERS
F-2/16, Ansari Road, Daryaganj, New Delhi-110002
☎ 011-23240026, 011-23240027 • *Fax:* 011-23240028
Email: info@vspublishers.com • *Website:* www.vspublishers.com

Regional Office : Hyderabad
5-1-707/1, Brij Bhawan (Beside Central Bank of India Lane)
Bank Street, Koti, Hyderabad - 500 095
☎ 040-24737290
E-mail: vspublishershyd@gmail.com

Branch Office : Mumbai
Jaywant Industrial Estate, 2nd Floor-222, Tardeo Road
Opposite Sobo Central, Mumbai - 400 034
☎ 022-23510736
E-mail: vspublishersmum@gmail.com

Follow us on:

All books available at **www.vspublishers.com**

© Copyright: V&S PUBLISHERS
Edition 2017

Printed at : Repro Knowledgecast Limited, Thane

Publisher's Note

V&S Publishers has always believed in the dictum that an apple a day doesn't just keep the doctor away, it can also improve memory. It truthfully agrees with the principle that from eating the right foods to knowing the right exercises, training your mind to become sharp isn't always about textbooks and tests. With this practical guide, you can improve your IQ in no time! Through various chapters the book explains many ways by which one can develop one's brainpower, observation, concentration, reasoning and analyzing powers. At the end of each chapter, there is a brief paragraph named Advice that guides the readers about how to read the chapters, the salient features of the chapter and how it will practically help in improving and sharpening one's memory.

The aim basically is to keep a note of the developments and transformations in the reader's mind, behavioural patterns and his entire personality as he proceeds reading one after another chapters. The author has kept the chapters precise and interesting.

V&S Publishers hopes that every reader would find the book useful in meeting the purpose for which it has been created in the first place.

Contents

Know Your Mind

To begin with the improvement of your memory power, first it is important to know the power of your mind and what all it can do for you. What capacity and strength you already possess and how you can develop it further for much greater achievements. In this chapter, we will discuss the working system of the mind only and not its hardware, that is the brain, or its mechanical setup. It is not of much relevance here.

Human mind is like a rubber-band. The more you use it or the more you stretch it, the sharper and the more capable it becomes to store and analyse greater amounts of information. On the other hand, if you do not use it

Today's Date: __ / __ / ____
(Kindly write with a Pencil)

or let it just idle away, then it becomes highly frustrated, demotivated and useless for ever. And the situation gets worse with the increase in age. Gradually, the thinking, the storing and the analytical abilities subside making the person confused, mentally sick and a liability for all.

The mind has to be trained on a continuous basis to keep it active and in a good working condition so that it keeps delivering the way we want it to. Positive thoughts and new ideas is the ideal food for it. In this way, it remains happy and also keeps the whole functioning of the body at optimum levels.

A positive attitude develops from a strong belief in yourself, your capabilities and your past experiences. Aging of your brain depends directly on your attitude as well as the way of your thinking in day-to-day life. If you remain happy and tension-free for most of your life, then your brain will be more young and healthy even in the older stages of your life. Hence, your mental energies will function like a young adult. It means thinking more clearly, learning and recalling faster, always.

A promise is required from you to yourself today. A dedicated and serious effort from your side is to be applied to the methods suggested in this book. No stress or any kind of worries is required at all. Good results can be obtained only when calmness and patience is observed. Though results will vary from person to person, hence, there should be no competition or copying. You can always improve with another try one after the other, if need be. You will have to put in more efforts with your understanding and as per the improvement of your memory.

Our mind is a genius in its own way. But it is highly underutilised. Not more than ten percent of the mind is used even by the most successful people in the world. Just think if you can increase the working capacity of your mind even by a few percentages only, then it can change your life tremendously. This book will guide you in this direction. Read it, understand it and then apply the techniques as per your own convenience and capacity. Again, I am repeating, please do not compete or copy any other person. Just be yourself, and the world will be yours very soon.

This world has witnessed a great number of intellectuals since time immemorial. There have been great scientists, scholars, mathematicians, artists, saints, spiritual gurus and the like who have harnessed their mind power to such an extent that they could deliver their services, wisdom, inventions and discoveries for the betterment of mankind. Some of them are Newton, Albert Einstein, Graham Bell, John F.Hopkins, Shakuntala Devi, Deepak Chopra and many others. The list is endless.

Exercising and practising on a continuous basis is required to keep the body and the mind fit. As a good and balanced diet with a regular workout is required to keep the body fit, similarly, feeding good, new and positive ideas from time to time are compulsory to keep the mind in optimum health. Physical exercises helps to keep the blood vessels in good condition, lowers cholesterol levels and opens-up blocked arteries as well. This further ensures regular supply of blood and oxygen to the brain. Hence better functioning of the mind.

Human mind is the most complex and the known most capable organ amongst all of the living entities. Mental exercises like playing games, solving puzzles, riddles and mathematical problems are considered good for keeping the mind healthy and active. When the mind is healthy then only it is wise and advisable to undertake any such activity, or schedule a program to enhance the memory power, so that it may not exert any kind of extra pressure on your mind and refrain you from taking due advantage of the memory enhancement program.

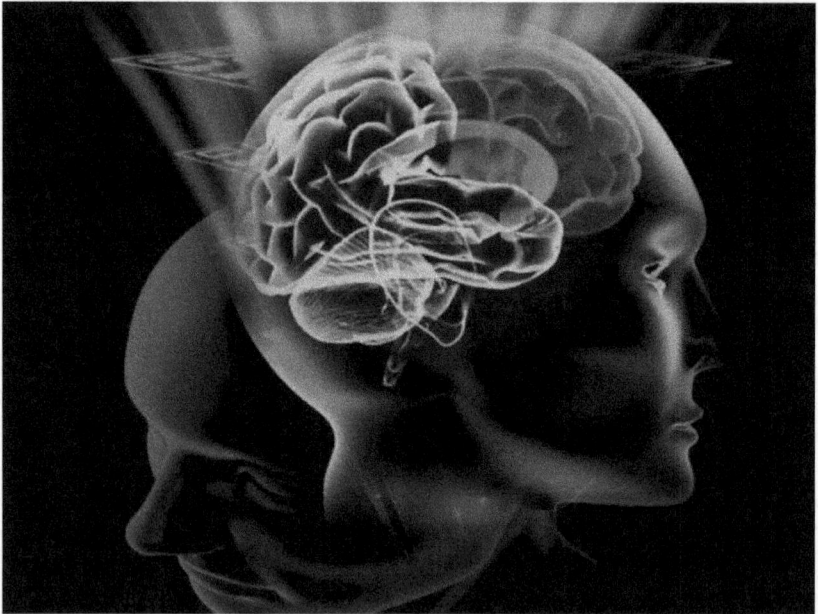

Make a fresh, new beginning in your life from today with great courage and motivation. This attitude will help you erase all your previous bitter experiences and memories. These could have become a potential deterrent in your new learning and during this Memory Enhancement Program.

Now, close your eyes, concentrate and visualise on what you wish to become in future. Do you wish to excel in your studies and be the most brilliant student, or you wish to be the best employee in your company? You may also be willing to be a topper in the Civil Services Examination or looking forward to a rewarding career in sales and marketing. The choices could be many as the choice is yours. This step – visualisation – is very important. Only then the techniques will work for you and give you the desired results.

Memory can be divided into two parts – short-term memory and long-term memory. Short-term memory records each and every thing that it comes across but for a short duration only. It can be momentary like remembering the story and its characters in a movie or a drama.

Long term Memory occurs in two ways. First, on its own, like a fearsome event that flashes across the mind later on and troubles all of us; the beauty and charm of a person which attracted us immensely and sometimes takes us back to that moment; the wonderful taste of a dish which we relished very much that it ticks us every time we come across good delicious food; a picnic spot, a waterfall or some other scenic beauty which had touched our heart, now flashed again while watching television, and so on. Second, when we deliberately repeat and rehearse our syllabus by reading or writing any text, speech, acts or songs, etc.

Functioning of the human mind can be divided into two parts which works simultaneously, the conscious mind and the subconscious mind. The subconscious mind keeps working even when we are asleep whereas the conscious mind somewhat comes to a rest. The subconscious mind controls the thought process of a person, his positive and negative emotions, his happiness and fears, analytical and learning abilities, etc. Hence, it becomes important for us to check every now and then what all is being fed to the mind. Because it itself cannot differentiate between the good and the bad. The subconscious mind will churn out the results only according to the data being supplied to it. And, accordingly it will also be responsible for the mood and emotions of the person.

It is a general known fact that our body or even a mechanical device starts to perform better whenever it is given a break or a rest in its working. The same is applicable to our mind as well. We generally feel refreshed and recharged after a good sound sleep. It happens because we had subjected our body and the conscious mind to rest for a few hours. This kind of sleep is more restful if taken during the night in complete darkness and silence. But as we wake up everything starts working automatically again. This is what we know as the recording and storing by the conscious mind.

Sleeping is a natural phenomenon undertaken by every human being where the body and the conscious mind are subjected to rest. And, that is why they remain in optimum health also. Night is the best time to sleep as our bodies are more attuned to work and rest according to the natural system of sunrise and sunset.

But what about the subconscious mind which has not been given rest for even a moment since our birth? And it is the subconscious mind that directly controls the analysis, the learning and the remembering processes. Proper nourishment, adequate rest and regular exercising are the keys to maintain a good health. Hence, it is our duty to give our subconscious mind good nourishment, necessary rest and exercises to enhance its capacity which in turn will improve your memory.

Nourishment

Nourishment to the mind can be provided in three ways. One, is by eating a balanced diet comprising the required vitamins, minerals, amino acids and other nutrients on a regular basis. Second, is to increase the supply of oxygen in the blood going towards the brain by doing some physical activities like walking or using a bicycle to a nearby grocery store, often using the stairs instead of the lift or by helping your elders in doing some household chores. Third, is to keep meeting positive minded and successful people and discussing with them their success stories, and also by attending other motivational seminars and events.

Rest and Relaxation

Rest and relaxation to the conscious mind is controllable and can be provided in numerous ways like cutting off from one activity and switching over to the other for a few minutes, sleeping or napping, playing, watching TV, switching between subjects, bathing, brisk walking in a nearby park, walking barefoot on moist green grass early morning or stretching exercises, fishing, gardening, etc.

On the other hand, our subconscious mind is uncontrollable and its workings cannot be stopped. But, by practising meditation on a daily basis its working can be slowed down to some extent. And gradually to a greater extent thereby giving our subconscious mind the much needed relaxation and rest, though for a few minutes only. Such kind of rest to the mind multiplies its capacity of working, learning and remembering in due course of time. Besides, there is another big benefit of meditation also. During the initial moments of meditation all the negative emotions, thoughts, experiences and events start getting deleted from the mind automatically. This helps the mind to unclutter itself in the most natural and easiest way. It further helps in greater concentration and hence, in enhanced learning and remembering abilities.

The subconscious mind is more powerful and it influences the conscious mind in daily activities and in important decision making as well. Therefore, with little practice, patience and continuous efforts, we can give directions to our subconscious mind to work according to us and deliver the desired results to us. Our subconscious mind does wonders whenever it is told in a proper way to increase the capacity of the mind towards its workings and learning abilities. And, unknowingly in a few days we are able to work more efficiently and for longer durations with negligible fatigue. So, always feed and direct your mind with good and positive thoughts. The real power and working capacity lie with the subconscious mind, whereas the conscious mind has little role in the learning and remembering activities.

Exercises

What walking does to the body, thinking does to the mind. Both the activities are spontaneous and of utmost importance for our healthy living. Physical and mental exercises, both, help us to keep fit, healthy and in good condition throughout our lives. Physical exercises and activities keep us physically and mentally healthy, and mental exercises and activities also keeps us physically and mentally healthy.

Physical exercises and activities tone up our body physically and in the process regulates the blood circulation which helps to carry more oxygen to the brain. Regulated supply of fresh oxygen to the brain helps to keep the mind calm and relaxed which helps it to work better and faster. Whereas mental exercises and activities keep the mind active and alert which enables it to work better and faster. This in turn helps to keep the body active and healthy because the body is controlled through the mind.

> **Advice:** Kindly read this chapter at least two to three times today with an interval of four hours minimum. This will prepare your mind and its energies towards the Memory Improvement Programme.

✳ ✳ ✳

Prepare Yourself for the Memory Improvement Program

Following are enlisted some of the mental exercises which can prove to be very helpful in keeping the mind active, alert, sharp and focussed besides calm and relaxed as well. These are very simple to learn, adopt, practise and perform in our routine lives.

Indulge Your Mind in Guesswork

These activities will enable the mind to think and act differently in a way which is new to it and it has never done such things before. And gradually, the thinking capacity will start to expand.

- Keeping your eyes closed, roam about in your room and recognise things like the study table, chairs, table lamp, dining table, centre table, flower pot, curtains, cupboard, TV, computer, music system, etc., with your hands only.

- Place some local currency coins in a box and try to recognise and differentiate them.

- Safely stand on a roadside and try to distinguish between the different vehicles passing by on the basis of their engine sounds and horns.

- Whenever in a park try to recognise various flowers as per their fragrances.

- Try to guess and cross check the change in temperatures at home and other places that you happen to visit.

- Try to bathe with your eyes closed. Follow and perform all the routine activities with your guesswork.

- With your eyes closed try to recognise what all has been served to you during your meals through its odour or as felt by your hands.

Today's Date: __ / __ / ____
(Kindly write with a Pencil)

Try Using 'The Other Hand'

(**Note:** If you perform most of your routine jobs with your right hand then try using your left hand as the main hand. And if you are using your left hand for undertaking most of your routine jobs then use your right hand as the main hand in the following exercises).

Most of the people use their right hand for doing their routine jobs in this world. It means their left brain is being used more and the right side of the brain remains idle for most of the time. Gradually, when we start trying to use our other hand, that would be the left hand here, then we are giving ourselves a chance to kick start in using our right side of the brain also. Using both of our hands will also save a lot of our precious time as well besides enhancing of our memory power. In this way, with the following activities we can increase the working and storing capacity of our mind.

- Try to play and get hold of the ludo dice, table tennis racquet, badminton racquet, carrom board striker, chess, etc., with the other hand.

- Try eating your meals with a spoon or writing, drawing or painting with a brush, playing a musical instrument, etc.,. with your other hand.

- Try to switch on your television, computer, laptop, air-conditioner, music system, etc., and also using their remote control devices with your other hand.

- Try combing your hair, shaving, brushing your teeth, brushing your shoes, dialling a number on the phone or mobile handset, etc., with your other hand.

- Try cutting, peeling or eating fruits and vegetables, preparing and cooking your food, washing utensils, gardening and watering the plants, cleaning and greasing your vehicle, etc., with your other hand.

- Also, try to change sides and directions. Like, change your side while getting onto your bicycle or other two-wheeler vehicle. This should be tried before the vehicle has started moving. Also try to kick-start it using the other foot.

> **Advice:** Kindly read this chapter at least two to three times today with an interval of four hours minimum, and practise the activities that have been suggested to you. It will not be easy but it could turn out to be interesting.

***

DAY 3

Observation, Reasoning and Analysis

The following activities will help you to mould your thinking process by carrying out such actions that are different from the normal way of your life. Such activities are termed as co-curricular activities and are also associated with our studies in some way or the other.

- Solve different kinds of puzzles. It could be mathematical calculations, crosswords or re-arrangement of words in English or any other language, general knowledge questions, etc.

- Participate in group plays, acting, song and dance competitions, debates and lectures, etc.

- Participate in science exhibitions and competitions, seminars, fairs, matches, fetes, games and sports held in your school or educational institution.

- Start a new hobby, like drawing or painting, sketching, writing articles or poems, stamps or coins collection or even learning a new language, etc.

- Observing plants or flowers, insects, birds or animals, and gathering information about their formation and existence.

- Reverse counting is also an interesting activity, like 10,9,8, … 1,0.

- In the beginning, see and count in reverse and after some time repeat the reverse counting verbally without seeing it written anywhere. Now gradually increase the counts, i.e. starting from 10 to reverse, then 20 to reverse and then 30 to reverse and so on.

- Imitate an actor, a celebrity or a famous personality for his acting skills, his other style or any other thing you like about him.

- Experimenting and playing games and sports in a

Today's Date: __ / __ / ____
(Kindly write with a Pencil)

different way or apply some new idea in using playing equipments like the balls, racquets, shuttle cock, dice, playing cards, etc. Try to throw up and rotate two or more balls by your hands.

☞ Try dribbling the basket ball or any other ball in a new way with both your hands at the ground as well as in the air or with a bat or a racquet.

General Precautions

☞ All activities should be undertaken with great care. Neither hurt yourself nor it should become a nuisance for others or look much absurd while practising.

☞ In the beginning some of the activities could appear to be boring or awkward or you may even fail in the early attempts as well, but these are going to enhance your memory to a great extent. So, patiently follow and practise them. Ultimately you are going to enjoy the benefits.

☞ These activities not only open up new avenues of thinking but also help to entertain, relax and refresh your mind as well.

☞ Undertake these activities in a rather joyful and playful mood. In this way it will become quite easy to grasp and practice with the new type of activities. It will not exert any extra pressure on the mind.

☞ And finally, the more you practice the better it will get with each passing day and gradually expand the capacity of your mind.

As you already know we humans seldom use even ten percent of our mind. Now think that when ten percent can do marvellous wonders in the world in inventions and discoveries in various fields like science and technology, space, medicine, computers, automobiles, telecom, etc., then think what can an enhanced capability of the mind can do towards the personal development of a person as well as towards the increased happiness of mankind.

> **Advice:** Practise all the activities at least three to four times today. Never mind about your performance or the failed attempts. It will get better with every next attempt.

✳✳✳

Develop Good Learning

Learning is a continuous process which happens in multiple ways. It starts with your very first breath since the birth itself. It is a natural phenomenon that your mind understands, learns and remembers logical facts more easily, and all those things that it comes across repeatedly. Hence, practising something regularly and repeatedly is surely bound to deliver better results. For this, observation power should also be good.

Natural Ways of Learning

Learning takes place through seeing and observing, touching, feeling and sensing, hearing, smelling, tasting and recognising. Whatever stage of sensing your body passes through is recorded in the mind immediately. And gradually, a database gets created of all that has been seen, heard or felt. This is a natural process of learning which will continue throughout your lives till the last breath.

Today's Date: __ / __ / ____
(Kindly write with a Pencil)

Formal Education

The other learning process begins with your formal education in the school, through normal teachings, coachings and other training programs undertaken during the school life or during professional upgradations. Whatever you read, hear, study or observe is recorded in the mind. Whenever you practise your course material time and again, it becomes ingrained in your mind with repeated learnings. But for proper understanding, good learning and recalling abilities, you need to have a good and sharp memory power.

Learning by Analysis

This kind of learning takes place when we get answers and solutions to our difficulties and problems. It is again a natural phenomenon that whenever we are confronted with a problem, we approach our mind and our mind starts to work out probable solutions at the subconscious level. The mind approaches and analyses the database and previous experiences. This process sometimes is able to give suitable solutions within a few seconds or may even extend to a number of days. Guessing is also an integral part of this process.

Here are a few examples

1. Many times, we try to guess and ascertain the timings during the day, be it early morning, the noon or the evening, whenever we are stranded without a watch or a clock nearby.

2. Sometimes, when all of a sudden, we have to visit an ailing relative in another city at odd hours, choosing the right mode of transport, be it public or private, becomes a matter of concern. We also have to consider about the safety and convenience of the people travelling with us, the approximate timing of reaching there, carrying a doctor along or any other relevant help, etc.

3. Analysis plays a major role in choosing the right life partner for marriage or even a business partner as well. We have to analyse and finalise as per our criteria and suitability from all the given facts and conditions mentioned.

It has been felt by many people that the mind works better and faster when it is in a relaxed state of mind. It generally gives incorrect ideas and answers when it is in tension or extreme pressure. So always try to remain calm and peaceful and also try to see the positive side of the situation. This will in turn help your mind to give you favourable solutions.

Learning by Hit and Trial Method

This is another common method of learning. Here learning takes place when you will continuously keep on solving a problem. Repeatedly keep on trying new ideas and techniques in old and new ways to be able to solve the problem. And soon you will start feeling comfortable in the given situation. The more you practise the better it will get. Moreover, you will also learn how to practise better with the next attempt.

A few examples are:

1. A very common situation arises while unlocking a door in the initial days when we are unable to find the right key for it in a bunch. The situation worsens when we are in a hurry. But, later on, with regular usage we are able to recognise the right keys for particular doors rather easily.

2. Similar situation arises with a light and switch board. In the initial days, it is hard to remember which switch is connected to which particular light, bulb or fan. But gradually, we are able to recognise the right switch button with more comfort and ease.

3. The same technique also comes into use when we are solving games and puzzles. It happens more with crosswords or while playing scrabble where various combination of words have to be formed and worked out.

There are various factors that influence the learning process in any person. The same is applicable to keep the information intact, accurate and for faster recalling. Hence, these methods are important afterwards also. They are as follows:

Willingness, Cheerful Mood and Positive Attitude

Learning is faster and more accurate when there is willingness, cheerful mood and positive attitude to practise or observe something. This is a natural phenomenon. Positive affirmations also help to keep intact and further develop positive attitude towards life in general.

Satisfaction Level

All those activities, assignments and subjects which are read and understood easily by the mind have a greater satisfaction level. And whenever and wherever the satisfaction level is good, the learning also tends to be good.

Inspiration

Inspiration comes from within and works wonders towards the learning process. A person gets inspired by the success and achievements of others. Then he also develops similar interests and feelings to focus and concentrate better and work harder towards his studies or work.

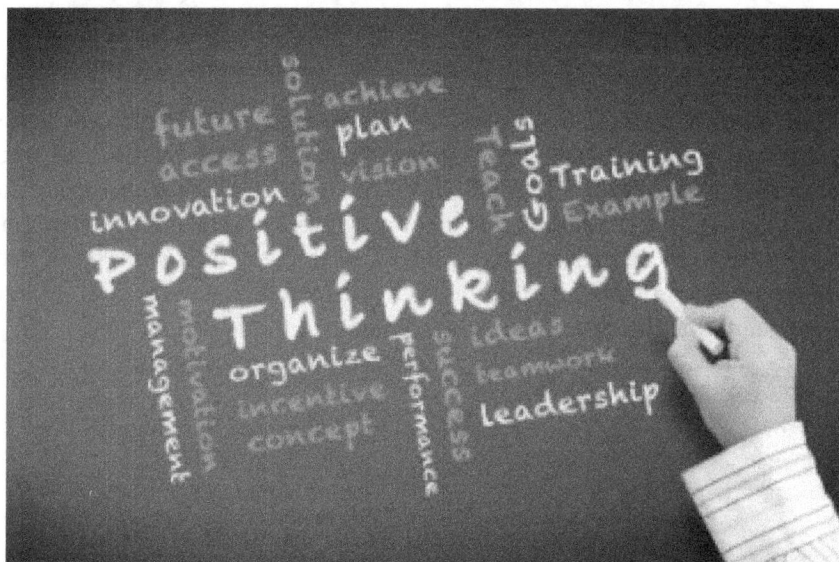

Motivation

A person feels motivated in undertaking an activity when he begins to visualise that he is an important part of the success story. Here the motivation takes place when a person thinks about his own achievements, whereas when he hears about other people's success, he feels inspired to work towards his goals.

Practice and Repetition

Practising and repeating the course material by reading and writing results into more accurate and faster learning. It also eliminates any chances of mistakes with regard to tenses, spellings, punctuation or grammar, etc. Pronunciation and communication of a language gets better with regular listening, reading aloud and conversing with other people.

Face Challenges Boldly

Whenever we start something new or afresh, we all come across certain types of problems, obstructions and challenges. It could be with regard to accepting and adopting the new activities and changes that starts taking place in our daily routine life. It may also demand a change in our lifestyle and thinking. These challenges could be laziness, un-readiness to adopt new ways of thinking, changes in living style or diet patterns, etc. It could also be certain type of fears or phobia or may arise on account of shortage of time and funds. But, remember that there are always ways and means to fulfil your desires. You only have to look, plan and work differently now to participate in new activities and get used to it.

Remain Active and Alert

Whenever we are active and alert in our approach, we tend to come across several new activities and events taking place around us. Such an approach also leads us to opportunities where we can develop our talents further and learn newer things. Despite our great learning, knowledge, achievements and success, there still remains millions of things which we are not even aware of. So, always be open to fresh and new ideas with an attitude to learn something new on a continuous basis.

> **Advice:** Kindly read this chapter at least two to three times today with an interval of four hours minimum. This will prepare your mind and its energies towards the Memory Improvement Programme.

✳✳✳

Develop Your Observation Power
Part - I

Good Observation leads to Good Analysis which further leads to Good Learning. Good observation can be initiated and developed quite easily. Noticing things and events more carefully and minutely results into good observation.

Let us take a look at a simple example:

A	HONESTYIS THE BEST POLICY	B	HONESTY IS THE IS BEST POLICY
C	HONESTY IS THE THE BEST POLICY	D	ONESTY IS THE BEST POLECY

Of the four boxes A, B, C, D shown above, only one box contains the correct phrase and the rest others are incorrect in some way or the other. Which one is the correct one and what are the mistakes in the other sentences? Kindly find it out for yourself and get it checked by your parents, teachers or any other elder person.

People having good observation are found to commit fewer mistakes as compared to other people. Good observation leads to good intellect which develops a cautious approach in a person forever. Such people tend to learn from their bad experiences as well as from the bad consequences faced for the mistakes and carelessness committed by other people.

Psychologists are also of the opinion that people having good observation power also have better intellect and good memory. Such people tend to learn things more

Today's Date: __ / __ / ___
(Kindly write with a Pencil)

quickly and are also able to retain it for longer durations and with greater accuracy. So, it becomes important for people to improve their observation power first. It is especially important for those who are slow or careless in observing even the simple things or events taking place around them.

Before taking up the exercises for improving your observation power, let us first prepare ourselves in the following ways:

- Start reading good detective stories and novels. Also start watching detective serials and movies. Detective works are based on observing minutest details of the place of crime, activities and emotions of the people related with the event, etc. This will not only help you but train you greatly in your observing and remembering process. This will also make you more cautious in your approach required in general day-to-day living.

- Start collecting information about the inventions and discoveries taking place around the world. A lot of hard work, dedication, patience, caution and minute observation are required to carry out all such activities. Try to find out and learn what were the techniques engaged and various methods adopted by the team involved. This will help you to develop your observation power to a great extent. Make a separate folder for each invention and discovery.

- In your school, office or place of work, try to get involved in activities or be a part of projects which require some kind of research or investigations necessary to accomplish the assignment. This will teach and train you about the techniques required to carry out the study.

Advice: Enquire from your friends or colleagues or from the nearby bookshop about the detective stories, books or novels available with them. Try to borrow such books on returnable basis only, at least in the beginning. Similarly, make enquiries about the TV series or movies based on detective stories. The choice is yours.

The idea here is to learn observation, and how these detectives observe and take into account the minutest of details in their investigations without missing out to note anything.

* * *

Develop Your Observation Power
Part - II

Here are some exercises to improve your observation power. You may maintain a diary for this purpose as well.

(To be carried out before you go to sleep at night, for at least one month.)

(Answers once written, should not be erased, altered or cancelled).

(With daily practice, accuracy will start happening on its own).

At what time you woke up in the morning? = ...

At what time you had your bath? = ...

At what time you had your breakfast? = ...

What all you had in your breakfast? = ...…..

What dress you wore today? =........................…..

What was the colour of your dress? =........................…..

Were you feeling comfortable in it? = Yes / No / Okay

Did you feel more confident today? =........................…..

Or did you feel lazy and tiresome today? =........................…..

How others judged you today? = Good / Better / Normal

What you liked about yourself today? =........................…..

What you disliked about yourself today? =........................…..

Advice: Maintain a daily record for at least six to eight months. This will greatly enhance your observation. Gradually, you will also come to know about what others are thinking about you.

***

Today's Date: __ / __ / ____
(Kindly write with a Pencil)

Practice Session - I

I hope you must have thoroughly read all the chapters till now. I also think that you must have followed the advice mentioned at the end of every chapter. I hope you must have started working on the methods suggested and must be enjoying them as well.

Today we will practise some of the exercises again (the exercises we have already practised. However, repeat these exercises to improve your memory further. Please don't ignore these exercises before we proceed further.) This is being done to assess your understanding, learning and development in this regard.

Indulge Your Mind in Some Guesswork

These activities will enable the mind to think and act differently in a new way as it may not do such things before. And gradually, the thinking capacity will begin to expand.

- Keeping your eyes closed, roam about in your room and recognise things like the study table, chairs, table lamp, dining table, centre table, flower pot, curtains, cupboard, TV, computer, music system, etc., with your hands only.

- Place some local currency coins in a box and try to recognise and differentiate them.

- Try to bathe with your eyes closed. Follow and perform all the routine activities with your guesswork.

- With your eyes closed, try to recognise what all has been served to you during your meals through its odour or as felt by your hands.

Try Using 'The Other Hand'

(**Note:** If you perform most of your routine jobs with your right hand, then try using your left hand as the main hand. And if you are using your left hand for undertaking most of your

Today's Date: __ / __ / __
(Kindly write with a Pencil)

routine jobs, then use your right hand as the main hand in the following exercises).

- 📷 Try to play and get hold of the ludo dice, table tennis racquet, badminton racquet, carrom board striker, chess, etc. with the other hand.

- 📷 Try eating your meals with a spoon or writing, drawing or painting with a brush, playing a musical instrument, etc. with your other hand.

- 📷 Try to switch on your television, computer, laptop, air conditioner, music system, etc. and also using their remote control devices with your other hand.

- 📷 Try combing your hair, shaving, brushing your teeth, polishing your shoes, dialling a number on the phone or mobile handset, etc. with your other hand.

- 📷 Try cutting, peeling or eating fruits and vegetables, preparing for and cooking your food, washing utensils, gardening and watering the plants, cleaning and greasing your vehicle, etc. with your other hand.

- 📷 Also, try to change sides and directions. Like, change your side while getting on to your bicycle or other two-wheeler vehicle. This should be tried before the vehicle has started moving. Also try to kick-start it using the other foot.

Mould Your Thinking

The following activities will help you to mould your thinking process by carrying out such actions that are different from the normal way of your life. Such activities are termed as co-curricular activities and are also associated with our studies in some way or the other.

- 📷 Solve different kinds of puzzles. It could be mathematical calculations, crosswords or rearrangement of words in English or any other language of your choice, general knowledge questions, etc.

- 📷 Start a new hobby, like drawing or painting, sketching, writing articles or poems, stamps or coins collection or even learning a new language, etc.

- 📷 Observing plants or flowers, insects, birds or animals, and gathering information about their formation and existence.

- 📷 Reverse counting is also an interesting activity, like 10,9,8, ... 1,0.

☞ In the beginning, see and count in reverse, and after some time repeat the reverse counting verbally without seeing it written anywhere. Now gradually increase the counts, i.e., starting from 10 to reverse, then 20 to reverse and then 30 to reverse and so on.

☞ Imitate an actor, a celebrity or a famous personality for his acting skills, his other style or any other thing you like about him.

☞ Try dribbling the basket ball or any other ball in a new way with both your hands at the ground as well as in the air or with a bat or a racquet.

Advice: Put a tick mark with a pencil in front of the activity you enjoyed doing it. You may also put a cross mark or mention a remark in front of the activity you could not perform correctly.

✻✻✻

Develop Your Observation Power
Part - III

OBSERVE

Take up any one of the following activities today to be a part of the improving your learning, remembering and recalling process. Rest of the activities should be taken later on to improve upon your observation power.

📹 Begin this with your own room first. Facing an empty wall, start writing down all the things, big or small, present in the room without looking back at them. When finished, now check it with all the things present in the room.

📹 Repeat the same exercise when you visit some public office, exhibition, museums, fairs, fetes, hotels and restaurants, etc. You may also note down their decorations at the entrance, on the floors, walls, roof or on the pillars, etc., and your opinions about it. Gradually, you will come to know the differences in the thinking of people from the various places visited.

📹 Repeat the same exercise when you visit your friend or someone in the neighbourhood. Upon return, note down all that you have noticed in their house, room, lobby or terrace. The idea is only to gauge the speed and accuracy of your observation. Now check your list when you visit them the next time. Judge your accuracy yourself. Now, you may either destroy or tear down the noting or simply hand

Today's Date: __ / __ / ____
(Kindly write with a Pencil)

it over to the respective house owner stating your good intentions in doing so.

📷 Similarly, whenever you happen to visit some other city, town, a village, countryside or even some other country, observe the people of that country. Also pay attention to their customs and rituals, language, currency, their way of living, etc. Such exercises will increase your observation power, your learning about new things as well as increase your memory power.

Advice: This is all for today. It may seem to be simple and small at the beginning, but it is time consuming. It will require a good deal of your energy and concentration as well. Hence, get started.

✳ ✳ ✳

Develop Your Observation Power
Part – IV

Below are mentioned some common activities to gauge your observation power. Taking up the following activities will make you more concerned even about the small things taking place around you.

☞ How many steps are there in the stairs of your building, your school, your college or your place of work and how these stairs are further sub-divided?

☞ You may also begin noticing and counting the stairs wherever you go. This will help you great extent in enhancing your observation and remembering skills.

☞ Prepare a record as to how much time was spent in various routine activities during the day, like waking up and leaving for school or office, time spent during travelling, in recreational activities, in relaxing or watching TV or spending time with friends, etc.

☞ Maintain a record of your income and earnings from other sources. Also prepare a chart of necessary and entertainment expenses.

☞ What is the normal time taken to reach the nearest bus stop, park or supermarket if you go walking, by your bicycle or by your car?

☞ How much time do you generally take to get ready when you are going to your school or office, to play, to the market or when going to attend

Today's Date: __ / __ / ____
(Kindly write with a Pencil)

some party or a function?

- Similarly, how much time do other members in the family take for all the activities stated above.

- With your eyes closed, try touching specific objects in your room, your house, certain plants and flowers in a garden, etc. If necessary, take someone's help to judge as well as protect you from getting hurt.

- Generally, what is your heart-beat or pulse rate when you have just woken up, back from school or office, after outdoor sports or exercising, after cooking or gardening, before and after meals, after prayers or meditation, etc.?

Advice: All these activities could seem to be somewhat awkward and absurd in the beginning, and noting down even more boring and wastage of time. But it will help you immensely in the long run.

Gradually, you will start noticing and recording the time consumed in various activities at the subconscious level. This in turn will help you in planning and managing your time more efficiently.

✳✳✳

Develop your Imagination
Part - I

Imagination is an activity of the mind of thinking about something which is non-existent. And it could also be about thinking something in a different format from its current shape or usage. Good imagination is the result of a well-nourished and a fertile subconscious mind. Good imagination has led to innumerable inventions, discoveries and other creative works throughout the world since time immemorial. Good imagination activates an astounding kind of courage and great mental strength within oneself.

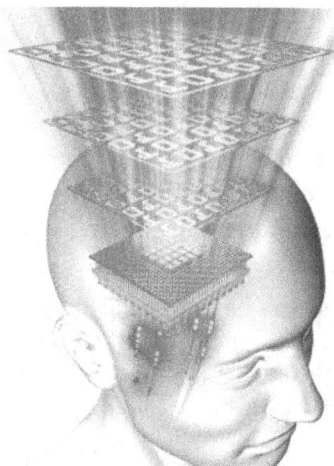

Good observation acts as a raw material for good imagination which helps a person to achieve and deliver great services beneficial for the mankind. Here meditation gives the subconscious mind the required fertilizers to process the desired results whenever an enquiry or requirement is fed to the mind.

All those people who possess or have developed their observation power and further strengthened their imagination are often able to deliver new kind of products and services. It could either be related to a new breakthrough in medicines, information technology, biotech, telecommunications, engineering, sports or even general goods and services.

All the people possessing good memory power are able to harness their mental energies

Today's Date: __ / __ / ____
(Kindly write with a Pencil)

effectively. They are also able to visualise their goals and plan out their working techniques in advance. This keeps them motivated enough which enables them to work continuously for hours and days altogether. They do not withdraw till they are able to make substantial improvements and achievements in their specific area of research. Without imagination and creative insights, it would be difficult to conceive new ideas as well as progress towards one's goals.

It is the power of good imagination and deep visualisation that many people are able to achieve their desired targets and positions in life. These positions can be in the field of education, sports or even in the office they work. The path towards success gets laid on its own. Only it has to be followed with honesty and devotion. Such methods have also led to personality development as well as happiness in relationships.

Visualisation of your goals is also one of the types of imagination of the results you wish to achieve. It greatly helps to keep the tedious process of hard work interesting and rather easy than being boring and cumbersome. The person also remains motivated. For a sportsman, for example, visualisation of achieving the No.1 position always plays a very important role towards his success besides all the hard work, practising and persistence that he has devoted to his game.

Visualisation of success works at the subconscious level giving a person an extra push, courage and extra strength of mind from within. It helps to break the normal thought process and enables him to emerge as a winner. That is why we often hear about new records being created either in the field of sports, higher percentages and rankings being touched in studies or a breakthrough achieved in some new research.

Imagination and visualisation of success have a small negative side also. But it is only for those who begin living in the world of day-dreaming, thus neglecting the basic facts and hard truths of the actual world. Many times people get lost in the yet-to-be-achieved success and its recognition thereof. They also start discriminating themselves as being superiors from the others. This greatly hampers their preparations for the development of their positive attitude. It also has a devastating bearing on their life if they happen to miss out or fail to achieve their desired targets. But, we must not forget that the technique of 'visualisation of success' works better when there are no rules, regulations or boundaries. Hence, due care should be taken in this respect.

Imagination is a natural system of your thought process. It is a continuous process wherein you may think or visualise anything randomly. Whenever good things or good ideas flash through your mind, you may start feeling good, happy or positive. But whenever your mind comes across some bad or negative thoughts or emotions, you may start feeling lonely, fearsome and demotivated towards life. Your good previous thoughts, experiences and happy moments lay the foundation for good imagination, and vice versa. Good imagination also leads to good planning. It is a psychological process which takes place on its own.

Imagination, many a times, can look to be absurd or meaningless. It is just a thinking or a weird guess. It has nothing to do with the actual logical world. But it is not the reality. Imagination can differ from person to person because each person has their own unique way of thinking. One person's experiences of life, observation, analysis and remembrance at the conscious and the subconscious level will also be different.

Our needs and desires also inspire the subconscious mind to think out of the box, i.e. to think or imagine differently. You must have certainly heard the famous saying: "Necessity is the Mother of Invention". Yes, this is very much true. Our necessities also give us a push to accomplish things in a different way every now and then. It is more prevalent in our daily routine lives as well. It is the inherent nature of human beings to lessen their burden of work and the time consumed in any process. Hence, the mind is continuously searching for new ways to simplify our workings. And the actual force gets developed from within, that is through our own imagination.

People with creative abilities are often found to either draw, paint, write or make different things to express their imaginations. And in the process, an idea might acquire the shape of a reality or an important invention. Like, for example, some person might have initially drawn the image of a man flying with his wings like a bird. Later on, Wright brothers went on develop a flying machine on similar pattern and thinking, though after a lot of hard work and trials. This ultimately resulted into one of the most important

inventions in the history of mankind. There are many more examples in this regard.

The automotive world in which we live in today and cannot do without has developed out of the need to simplify our day-to-day workings. Machines have decreased our physical labour substantially as well as made our lives more comfortable. It has also saved a lot of our hard pressed and precious time.

A few common examples are washing machines for clothes and dish washer for utensils; ceiling or table fan to give us the feeling of a breeze; an air conditioner which changes the temperature of the room or a building to protect us from heat; a heater to protect us from cold; a juicer which squeezes juice out of fruits faster for us to consume; a grinder which crushes various eatables to smaller units in only a few seconds; a grinder in a flour mill which turns wheat into flour which is further baked into making bread and other eatables, etc. Now you can yourself analyse the world around you and judge for yourself the importance of good imagination.

Similarly, the following examples also might have been the result of someone's imagination or creativity –

- A car, bus, train, boat, ship or an aeroplane carrying many people in a single journey
- A double-decker bus, train or an aeroplane with more seating capacity
- A rocket carrying people to space
- A metro train plying along with other traffic in the city
- Working in shifts in an office or a factory as per one's convenience with the help of time punching machines
- A zoo where we can safely see many of the big and other dangerous animals found in the forest
- A match stick, a stove lighter, a candle, etc. used in the kitchen
- A pencil, an eraser, a sharpener, an ink pen or a ball pen, etc., are different easy-to-use tools for writing
- A blackboard or a chalk used in a school
- A television or radio to entertain us
- A refrigerator to keep and preserve eatables at a colder temperature
- Live telecast of a program or a sports match being played miles away on radio, television or the internet

☞ Blending of Ethanol, a sugarcane by-product, and mixing it with petrol; and research work on other renewable energy sources and so on...

> **Advice:** Read this chapter at least three to four times during the day. The more the better. This will leave a deep mark on your mind with respect to the workings of imagination. This will also help you to gain an upper hand and self-confidence during this memory improvement program.

✱✱✱

Develop your Imagination
Part – II

Though developing your imagination power is somewhat a tricky matter, the following examples will help you to look, think and analyse the world around you in a different way. These may look awkward, funny or absolute foolishness at first, but as I said earlier also, it is just another way of thinking or merely a weird guess. Who knows, some of you might create something useful, interesting or entertaining out of it someday.

- For Men – Think about a man around you who is a thorough gentleman who dresses well, has good habits and takes care of his family and responsibilities well. Now, imagine that you are gradually adopting his good habits and are now feeling more confident.

- For Women – Similarly, think about a woman who is perfect in your opinion. Who takes care of her family well and manages the upkeep of her house as well as herself very well. Now, imagine that you are also beautiful, possess good dressing sense and are being looked upon by others more respectfully.

- On a day when you are feeling extremely tired, worried or de-motivated, think about your favourite movie or sports star, a scientist or a successful businessman. Now, imagine yourself to be similarly confident, happy and contented. Soon, you will be surprised to feel a sudden gush of strength inside you surrounded by positive energy all around.

- Imagine and create a new tune on a musical instrument for an existing favourite song or for a nursery rhyme you had liked.

- Try to develop a new recipe or prepare a commonly known dish in a new way by your imagination. You may also imagine to recall the taste

Today's Date: __ / __ / ____
(Kindly write with a Pencil)

about some dishes you had appreciated in the past.

- 🐦 Imagine about automobiles that use air pressure, salty ocean water or other liquid – partly or solely to operate.
- 🐦 A car which may ply on the road, fly in the air as well as swim in water.
- 🐦 Imagine about a new spaceship that would ferry more passengers in lesser time to the moon.
- 🐦 Imagine to clear the snow on roads with the heat of your vehicle's engine.
- 🐦 Think of developing new kind of life jackets which are bigger and much lighter to save larger number of people during floods.
- 🐦 Think of developing other additional uses of the mobile phones, television remote control devices or their batteries, etc.
- 🐦 Think about new methods of recycling of used, torn or worn out clothes, shoes, items made of paper or wood, etc.
- 🐦 Also, think of using minimal energy sources and creating lesser wastage in the process. And so on…

Sometimes you will have to work in a silly way also to create something different out of your imagination. Just start doing and your mind will guide you further.

Caution: You shoulod not think of doing something that goes against nature or harm plants and animals in any way. It should also not be against the law of the land or the society. That would be the negative side of your imagination.

✳✳✳

Improve Your Decision-Making Power

Decisions are the commands that are passed on to the mind to initiate action in order to fulfil the desired objectives. Decisions are an integral part of our lives. Our mind takes scores of decisions every now and then to think, act or move forward.

Some of the decisions are prompt that are taken in our daily routine life which begins from the very moment we wake up. These could be the choice of dress to be worn on that day, a specific breakfast, the mode of transport, calling certain friends or clients while travelling, drinking tea, coffee or a cold drink to keep oneself refreshed and so on. There are endless decisions we take that we even do not notice but they are somehow, automatically initiated by the mind and acted upon.

There are some decisions that are taken for short term, medium term and long term as well. Short term decisions could be regarding a crash course helpful along with the current studies, choosing a holiday destination for the upcoming vacations, making arrangements for birthday, anniversary or bachelor party next month and so on.

Medium-term decisions could be regarding taking up a hobby course, changing a job, taking up a

Today's Date: __ / __ / ____
(Kindly write with a Pencil)

new assignment or enrolling for a management program along with the existing job for upgradation, renovation or extention to your house and so on.

Long-term decisions are those which will affect you throughout your life. Such decisions could be choosing the stream of studies you wish to pursue like engineering, medicine, business studies or humanities. It could also be while choosing an interest for your livelihood like singing, acting, writing or even contesting elections to serve the people of your country, migrating to some other state or country permanently or with regard to choosing the right life partner for your marriage, etc.

Decision making is not an easy process for everyone. Many a times, people come across several doubts, such as if(s) and but(s) that it confuses them completely and renders them hopeless and clueless as what decision would be the most suitable for them. A few examples are:

- 📬 What *if* I did not feel comfortable in wearing cotton clothes today?
- 📬 It would have been better *if* I could take my car to the office today.
- 📬 Though I am preparing for the exams myself *but* coaching would also have been beneficial.
- 📬 I would have felt better *if* I had taken some tomato soup instead of a cup of coffee just before lunch time.
- 📬 I could have slept better *if* I had taken a bath before sleeping *but* could have caught cold as well.
- 📬 It would have been better *if* I had also studied law after graduation.
- 📬 How would I survive in another country *if* I could not get a suitable job or work? And so on...

All those people who have developed and trained their minds since their early childhood are more apt in solving such issues quite easily. It further paves the way for their success because they do not get stuck up easily like others. They courageously move forward towards accomplishing their goals. Doubts demotivate people very badly and have devastating effects on their lives. Previous experiences and sharpness of their minds help people in overcoming their doubts and they are able to move forward in life confidently.

Self-confidence is a positive step in this direction. People holding high positions and in-charge of other authoritative designations are found to have greater amount of self-confidence as well as higher intellectual powers because decisions taken by such people will affect a large number of people of their company, their society or their nation as a whole. Hence, intellectual powers should be improved and enhanced so that you can take your decisions more speedily and accurately. A decision once taken should be implemented immediately without much delay or doubt. Otherwise, the objective of the decision would fail to deliver the desired results.

Methods to improve your decision-making abilities:

- Start maintaining a small notepad or a pocket diary with the current year dates with yourself always.

- Now, as per the dates printed on the diary, after thinking carefully, start noting down the works and pending assignments as per the availability of your time and convenience.

- A work once mentioned on a certain date should be undertaken on that date itself without any kind of delay due to laziness or mood swings.

- Before taking any decision, you must ensure your objective very well. Then only the work will begin and be implemented properly.

- Always seek and hire the advice and services of a professional like an advocate, a chartered accountant or a doctor wherever required.

- Besides the above professional help, you must also equip yourself with the information from other sources for your own knowledge. It will help you in taking decisions more effectively.

- Refer your previous decisions and experiences thereof in taking decisions. It is quite possible that you are confronted with similar types of problems in your field of weaknesses and shortcomings.

- Also, try to analyse and solve problems with a different perspective. Such an approach also works wonders.

- First, calmly try to understand the problem in its actual sense that is troubling you, then only work on finding its solution.

- A written down approach is a better way than analysing and solving problems verbally. Make a separate list for everything. Like for things available and for things that are short, etc. It will avoid any kind of unnecessary burden on your mind.

Precautions

- Never take decisions in haste.
- Relaxation also proves a boon while taking decisions. Sometimes postponing a decision for some time is quite helpful.
- Never take decisions due to shortage of time.
- Never take decisions when you are being pressurised by others.
- Never take decisions without analysing each and every aspect of the concerned subject matter.
- Never take decisions in a state of intoxication.
- Never take decisions while you are feeling tired, worried or feeling drowsy.
- Never take decisions when you are very busy in some other work or while talking with somebody.

Your decisions should not only be fruitful to you, but also be acceptable by the society you are living in. Your decisions should never work against the interests of the common man. Otherwise, the negative effects of the same will certainly affect you and your family any time in future. Hence, take due considerations with enough time and intelligence while taking decisions.

> **Advice:** Read this chapter at least three to four times during the day, today.

✱✱✱

Improve Your Concentration Part - I

'Concentration' means to devote all your energy and efforts in getting a certain work completed without any kind of distractions or disturbances. It enables faster learning in lesser time with good understanding of the subject matter. Along with firm determination, it further helps our minds to work better towards storing and recalling information at a later date.

Human mind is the most powerful organ amongst all the other forms of living entities in this world. It has great power and capabilities hidden inside it. Our mind undertakes multiple tasks every second. Its power is immeasurable. Hence, when the mind is focussed on a single task, it is able to deliver astonishing results. All great scholars, scientists and other successful people undertake their tasks with full zeal, determination and most importantly, concentration.

Today's Date: __ / __ / ____
(Kindly write with a Pencil)

Methods to Improve Your Concentration and Focus

- Wherever you are sitting or standing alone or in a queue, close your eyes, take a deep breath slowly and release it slowly. Repeat this 5-10 times. This will always help to calm you down and help focusing your mind.

- You may undertake this activity several times during the day. This will ensure a small rest to your mind and further help it to work better.

- Undertake only one activity at a time whenever possible. Accomplish your tasks one by one.

- Do not let your mind wander away from the task at hand. Finish it first, then only you may look at other things.

- Always use a stable table and chair while studying. This greatly helps to improve your concentration and avoid any kind of disturbances.

- Always use good quality stationery. In this way, the distractions are minimal and hence, you can focus better on your work.

- Developing good understanding and interest in the subject matter also helps in improving concentration, and vice versa.

- Devise your own ways of creating interest in studies or works that seem to be boring or of lesser interest to you. Take the help and guidance of seniors and other successful people in that particular field.

- Always wear neat and clean clothes to feel comfortable and hence, focus better on your work.

- Always take lighter meals preferably 4-5 times during the day instead of 2 or 3 heavy meals. This not only ensures optimum health but also results into better concentration.

- Try to avoid too much oily, spicy, cold or fast food. These foods also make you lethargic and unhealthy which results into a lot of distractions.

- Prefer home-cooked food most of the time. And eat food when it is being served hot. It enables good digestion, good health and good concentration.

- Regular bathing also refreshes and energises the body and mind together. It greatly relaxes and calms the mind and helps to concentrate better.

- Use natural light for most of the time. Using artificial light for long durations stresses the mind more and disturbs concentration and learning.

- Never compromise on your sleeping hours. Instead lessen your time being spent on sports, entertainment, travelling, part-time job or even for your studies. An adequate hours of sleep ensures enough rest to the mind, hence better concentration and remembrance.

- Pending works and assignments are a big burden and distraction for the mind. Hence, try to finish your tasks as per your time table and schedules.

- It is often felt by many that whenever a task is done in a special way or given extra importance, the results are found to be more positive and encouraging. Hence, attach a special purpose to almost all the tasks that you are responsible for.

- Adopt and follow a simple and positive attitude towards life. Because dishonesty is the most disturbing emotion for the mind. It will also help you to control your bad habits, if any, and also overcome other shortcomings.

- Our mind believes what we make it to believe and feed into it. Hence, feel and act as if you are calm and relaxed before starting any task. It will direct the mind to focus better on the given task.

- Try to choose the right time and atmosphere to start up any new assignment. A good start will ensure good progress. Convenient and suitable timings during the day will vary from person to person. Some people prefer morning hours whereas some prefer late evenings. It also depends on the kind of activity you wish to take up.

Advice: Read this chapter at least three to four times during the day today.

***

Improve Your Concentration Part - II

The following examples will help you to understand better the concept and importance of concentration. Whenever we watch a good movie starring our favourite actors, we tend to remember the story, the sequences and even the dialogues for a long time. It so happens because we had devoted our full concentration in the movie. Similarly, while playing our favourite game or sport, we generally tend to win the game because we were playing with full, concentration. In both the instances, our mind records even the smallest of details carefully which enables good memory and hence, 'success'.

Exercises to Improve Your Concentration and Focus:

- **Meditation:** Though it is done in various ways around the world, here we will

Today's Date: __ / __ / ____
(Kindly write with a Pencil)

discuss the two ways only which are the most appropriate. It can be done with your eyes closed as well as with your eyes open.

- **Meditation with eyes open:** Sit or stand still and focus your eyes on a fixed object which is 2-3 metres away from you. These objects could be either a wall hanging, a painting or a photo, a black dot measuring a small currency coin, a lamp or a burning candle. The black dot or the lit candle should be preferred.

- **Meditation with eyes closed:** Sit still and straight with legs crossed over each other. Now take a slow, deep breath inside. Now exhale your breath slowly. Repeat it 3-5 times. Keep sitting still, calm and idle. During this time you are neither supposed to talk, do anything or think about anything.

- Just sit idle and silently. Do not try to focus on anything. There is only darkness and peace inside. So, sit still, and feel and enjoy the peace. Now you are one of the few people who have found peace inside yourself and have got connected with it as well.

- Preferably meditate in a silent place where there is minimal or no disturbance of any kind. This is especially important in the initial days of practice. And if there happens to be some kind of noise don't feel disturbed or distracted. Along with your meditation, try to enjoy and absorb this noise. Let it just pass through your mind. Do not ever try to stop it from entering your mind. Because stopping it will only disturb you. So, it is better to let it pass through you. In this way you will be able to keep yourself more relaxed and undisturbed paving the way for eternal bliss.

- Having practised the previous stage, now you have trained your mind to meditate anywhere. It could be either in the bus or train while travelling, waiting at the bus stop, station or even inside a restaurant, at the beach, at the riverside or in a park. You may also concentrate on the sound of waves and a waterfall nearby or get surrounded in the beauty of nature.

- As per your location and convenience, focus your eyes and mind on a certain object which is still, that is which is not moving. It has two great benefits. One is that you are utilising your free time in meditation and increasing your concentration power. And secondly, you are saving yourself from getting bored. Lonliness can provoke you to think negatively as well as you may indulge in some activity which can prove to be injurious to you. Like you may feel the urge to smoke, stare at someone, overeating or even chatting with somebody unnecessarily.

- Meditation is a method to give rest to the mind. Here you are trying to cut off the link of the mind engaged in active thinking, planning or in executing some task. Gradually, with regular practice of 10-15 minutes only everyday, your mind gets used to switching itself off from active thinking and working, and starts feeling relieved and relaxed. Automatically, the time being devoted towards meditation will itself get increased. In that case, you may start using an alarm clock which will alarm you, say after every 20, 30 or 45 minutes.

Advice: Read this chapter at least three or four times during the day. Begin meditation straightaway.

✳✳✳

Practice Session - II

Learning by Hit and Trial Method

As we have already discussed earlier, this is another common method of learning. Here learning takes place when you will continuously keep on solving a problem. Repeatedly, keep on trying new ideas and techniques in old and new ways. The more you practise, the better it will get. Moreover, you will also learn how to practise and learn better with every next attempt.

Exercise 1: Prepare a bunch of all the keys that are being used in your house in a common key ring. Lock out all the possible doors and drawers, etc. in your home. Now, start unlocking all the doors and drawers one by one. With the help of your watch, note down the total time taken in a diary. Repeat this activity once every week.

Exercise 2: Locate a big light and switch board having at least 15-20 switches or more in your house, office or a nearby community centre, etc. First, recognise all the respective switches with their respective connections. Switch off all the switches. Now, close your eyes for a minute, take and release a deep breath 3 times and calm your mind down. Now, open your eyes and start switching on the switches. Note down all the right and wrong attempts in a diary. Repeat the same activity once every week.

In both the exercises above, also judge and mention your performance. The reasons for good performance and the reasons for poor performance on that day. Also, observe the improvements taking place after every month.

Check Your Observation

With the help of the following examples, check and judge your observation power in the first attempt. Only one of the following sentences is correct. Find out and tick the correct one with a light pencil. Also, mark out the mistakes in the other sentences. Kindly find it out for yourself and get it checked by your parents, teachers or any other elder person.

Today's Date: __ / __ / ____
(Kindly write with a Pencil)

Example 1:	A. HONESTY IS THE BEST POLICY.
	B. HONESTY IS THE BEST POLICY
	C. HONESTY IS THE BEST POLICY
	D. ONESTY IS THE BEST POLECY

Example 2:

A. EARLY TO BED EARLY TO RISE MAKES A MAN HEALTHYY, WEALTHY AND WISE.

B. ERLY TOO BED ERLY TO RISE MAKE A MAN HELTHY, WELTHY AND WISE.

C. EARLY TO BAD EARLY TO RIS MAKES MAN HEELTHY, WEELTHY AND WIS.

D. ARLY TO BED ARLY TO RISE MAKS A MAN HEALTHY, WELLTHY AND WYSE.

Example 3: Check out the lists prepared earlier and make new additions to it.

Detective Stories, Novels or Movies / or Related with Research			
S.No.	Read/Watched	Reading/Watching	Planned
1.			Sherlock Holmes
2.			Hardy Boys
			Nancy Drew
3.			by Alfred Hitchcock
4.			The Old Fox
5.			Project UFO
			Star Trek
6.			James Bond Movies
7.			Discovery Channel,
			Animal Planet, etc.
			and so on…

Detective works are based on observing the minutest details of the place of crime, activities and emotions of the people related with the event, etc.

Similarly, research and discovery related projects also show the minutest sequence and progress of their research works. Start collecting information about the inventions and discoveries taking place around the world. Try to find out and learn what were the techniques engaged and the various methods adopted by the team involved.

This will train you greatly in your observing, learning and remembering process. This will also make you more cautious in your approach required in general day to day living as well.

Also, enquire from your friends, colleagues or from the nearby bookshop about the detective stories, books or novels available with them, and other such materials related with research and discoveries available with them. Try to borrow such books on returnable basis, at least in the beginning.

Similarly, make enquiries about the TV series or channels.

Other Ways to Improve Observation

Take up any one of the following activities one by one. It will help you in improving your learning, remembering and recalling process.

- Start this with your own room first. Facing an empty or any one of the walls, start writing down all the things, big or small, present in the room without looking back at them. When finished, now check it with all the things present in the room. Repeat this in every month.

- Undertake the above activity when you visit some public office, exhibition, museums, fairs, fetes, hotels and restaurants, etc. Gradually, you will come to know the differences in the thinking of people from the various places visited. It is especially useful for frequent travellers.

- Undertake the activity when you happen to visit your friend or someone in the neighbourhood. Upon return, note down all that you have noticed in their house, room, lobby or terrace. Now check your list when you visit them the next time. Judge your accuracy yourself.

- Count how many steps are there in the stairs of your building, your school, your college or your place of work.

- You may also start noticing and counting the stairs wherever you go. This will help you greatly in enhancing your observation and remembering skills.

- What is the normal time taken to reach the nearest bus stop, park or supermarket if you go walking, by your own vehicle or by some public transport.

- How much time do you generally take to get ready when you are going to your school or office, to play, to the market or when going to attend some party or a function.

- Similarly, how much time do other members in the family take for all the activities stated above.

- Generally what is your heart beat or pulse rate when you have just woken up in the morning, back from school or office, after outdoor sports or work-outs, after cooking or gardening, before and after meals, after prayers or meditation, etc.

Advice: You may sub-divide the activities as per the availability of your time. Such activities are meant to enhance your memory power but at the same time, it should not disturb your daily schedule.

***

What is Memory?

Memory is an important function of the brain without which our existence can come to a standstill. It further comprises three important inter-connected sub-functions. These are Learning, Remembering and Recalling of the information. All these three functions work simultaneously and in tandem with each other. Let us try to understand how all these work.

Each and every moment our mind is recording all the activities that we come across. It could either be by reading, writing, seeing, feeling, smelling, hearing, interacting and so on.

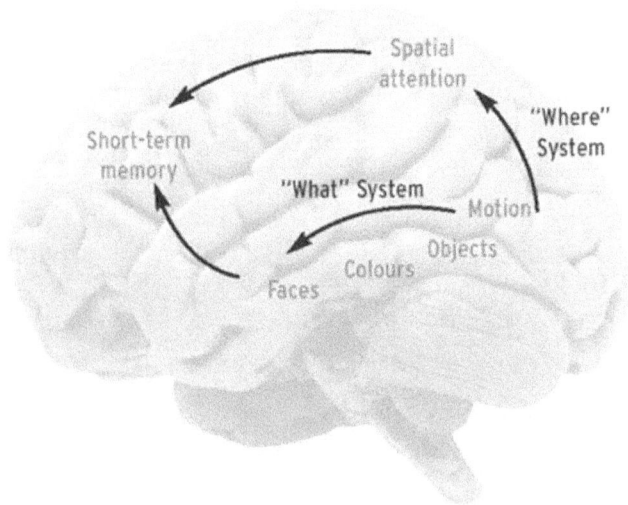

When any activity clicks, it gets noticed or it leaves an impression on the mind and thus *Learning* takes place. When an activity or an event gets repeated or gets stored in the mind it is known as *Retention or Remembering*. It is a natural phenomenon. And lastly, when any such stored information is required the process of *Recalling* is

Today's Date: __ / __ / ____
(Kindly write with a Pencil)

activated by the mind.

Retention of any information can be temporary or for short term and permanent or for longer term. It can also be called short term memory or long term memory respectively. Let us now understand these two characteristics of memory power in a bit more detail.

Short-Term Memory

Any such information that is retained by the mind for a few minutes to a few days and further for a few months only is known as short term memory. In most of the cases we know from the very beginning that the required information will be used in the short term only. Hence, when the stated event happens or by the time the objective gets fulfilled the mind automatically starts to forget all the things gradually, and new things are captured by the mind.

Examples of Short-Term Memory:

- Your travel and lodging details while going on a holiday or for attending a seminar with a delegate out of town. Like your date and timing of travel, your seat no. on the bus, train or airplane you would be travelling by, and similarly for the return journey as well. And your room no. in the hotel or guest house you will be staying and its name.

- Again all the similar details if you happen to visit more than one city during the same trip.

- Subjects and syllabus studied during the whole year is learned, remembered and retained by the mind during the year itself. But, as soon as the final exams are over and we are promoted to the higher class, most of the learned information is lost. And it is taken over by the fresh syllabus. Only the formulas, methods and techniques are retained.

- When we are working on a certain project or assignment the mind learns and remembers all the terms, conditions and directions important to run the project effectively. But as soon as the project is over, gradually our mind tends to forget the details with the passage of time. And, again it is taken over by the new guidelines of the new assignment.

Long-Term Memory

Any such information that is retained by the mind for a longer duration extending from a few years to the entire lifetime of a person is known as long term memory. These are the formulas and techniques that we generally learn during our studying years or while working in the professional domain as well. As per our way of thinking and attitude towards life, we constantly give directions to our subconscious mind about the importance of the information we are coming across, and accordingly our mind remembers those things for a longer duration. All such things once learnt may be applied for several times in your life.

Examples of Long-Term Memory:

- Formulas of mathematics, grammar, punctuation and tenses of any language; laws of scientific or fundamentals of physics and chemistry, and so on.

- Remembering birthday and anniversary dates of your near and dear ones. It helps in maintaining good relationships all around.

- Learning for yourself or by simply observing other people repairing household goods or even tending to small problems with your vehicles. These could be as simple as fixing the blades of a juicer or grinder in the kitchen, mending the fuse in the electricity box of your house, tightening of loose wires in the plug or switch, soldering the broken wires of your electric iron, changing the punctured wheel of your motorbike or car, and so on.

- Cooking food starting with simple things first. Like boiling of water or milk for preparing tea or coffee, and gradually, adding other ingredients to prepare the desired dish or beverage. Butter toast, sandwich and omelette is a very common breakfast which is eaten and cherished worldwide.

- Learning good etiquettes, manners and behaviour is also an important part of our daily life. These are mostly learnt by good observation and is useful throughout life.

Exercises for the Day:

- To properly understand what all has been told above, kindly prepare two separate lists. One list will be for the past and the other will be for the future.

- Now divide both these two lists further into two sections each namely short term and long term.

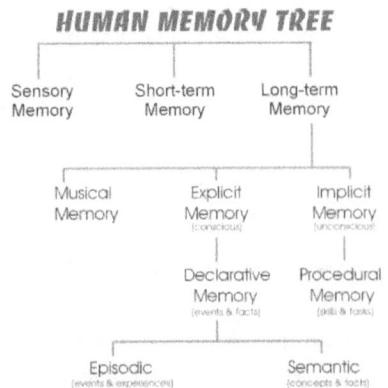

HUMAN MEMORY TREE

Sensory Memory — Short-term Memory — Long-term Memory

Musical Memory — Explicit Memory (conscious) — Implicit Memory (unconscious)

Declarative Memory (events & facts) — Procedural Memory (skills & tasks)

Episodic (events & experiences) — Semantic (concepts & facts)

- In the Past list – long-term section, write down all the events, activities and information that you remember from your childhood and teenage days, e.g. your first day at school or the day you went to buy your first bicycle or skates; when you stood first in your class or when you won the race on sports day; your first love and so on.

- In the Past list – short-term section, write down all the events, activities and information that you remember from the recent past, e.g. a new friend or colleague whose friendship you like the most; or you were promoted, given a raise in salary or awarded a medal for your accomplishments; your decision to buy a car on your previous birthday, and so on.

- In the Future list – long-term section, write down all the events, activities and information that you feel would be required for the rest of your life, e.g. keep safely all the photographs of yourself and your family clicked during family functions; a big desk diary to note down the important events of life like birthdays and anniversaries of family members and friends or colleagues, etc. and so on.

- In the Future list – short-term section, write down all the events, activities and information that you feel would be required for a few months only., e.g. carefully retain the documents and bills of the new TV and juicer purchased for free repairs during the warranty period; other documents of incomes and major purchases which could be required by the taxmen, and so on.

FROM THE PAST		
S.No.	**LONG-TERM**	**SHORT-TERM**
1.	first day at school	a new friend met last year
2.	parents giving in to my persistent demand for a new bicycle	migrating to another city for studies only
3.		
FOR THE FUTURE		
S.No.	**LONG-TERM**	**SHORT-TERM**
1.	construction of own dream house	a small hike in salary for good work done

2.	admission to MBA with weekend classes	scholarship granted for higher studies
3.		

You can keep adding and re-arranging the list as per your liking and convenience on a regular basis as well. But try to complete a major part of these lists today itself to give it a good start. This will help you a lot to understand the working of our minds.

Written down approach is the best technique to increase your memory power. If you can develop the habit of writing down the important things of life in a diary, I can assure you that you will soon develop a memory that would be at par with the most intellectual people of this world. So, start today itself. Maintain a good quality desk diary for long-term usage and a small pocket diary for short-term usage. You will yourself feel the difference in a few days from today onwards.

> **Advice:** Read this chapter at least three to four times during the day today.

✳✳✳

How to Overcome 'Forgetting'?

What is Forgetting?

Inability of the mind to recall information is known as 'forgetting'. It may either be complete or partial. Forgetting Completely happens when we are not at all able to recall things which we may have used or come across earlier. Forgetting Partially means when we are able to recall some part of the things, but not everything.

We will try to understand these two types of 'forgetting' with the help of the following examples:

- Forgetting Completely happens when we fail to recall something we had read or learnt earlier or visited a place like a temple, a museum or a picnic spot. We may also fail to recognise a school time friend or an accomplice with whom we had worked previously on an assignment.

- Forgetting Partially takes place when we come across a person and recognise him as well but are not able to recall his name or as to where we had met earlier. This is a very common instance of partial recognition.

- Forgetting takes place in a third way also. When some other person recognises us and we are not able to recognise him. But when that person uses certain references with respect to some common friends or the places we had visited together or some

Today's Date: __ / __ / ____
(Kindly write with a Pencil)

other moments, we both had enjoyed together during the execution of a project, etc., we start recognising that person.

Importance of Forgetting

As we all know that our mind comes across numerous activities and things every moment. We also know that learning, remembering and forgetting is a naturally occurring continuous process. Forgetting old things is as important as learning new things.

Forgetting declutters the mind, eliminates and automatically deletes various subjects and issues in due course of time. Forgetting empties the space required for storing fresh information. Moreover, it also helps to avoid any such unimportant things from interfering in our day-to-day life, and helps in keeping the good memory intact.

Hence, it becomes utmost important for us to train our minds in such a way that it automatically filters and forgets all the irrelevant things from the mind, and makes more space for new and other important things. This is the basic difference between intellectuals and slow learners. All intellectuals and learned people have two things in common. One is, that they have trained their minds to learn faster and filter the trivial things successfully. And secondly, that they work harder and practise more than other people till the time they have properly learned the requisite skills.

Reasons for Forgetting

There are numerous reasons for forgetting. But with little efforts and careful handling of the affairs of daily routine life, the habit of forgetting and poor remembrance can be taken care of very effectively. It is not so difficult as has been considered by many. Children often tend to forget many small things during their examination days. Candidates appearing for an interview suddenly develop cold feet, start trembling or sweating. Psychologists have pointed out the following reasons:

- Disinterest, disregard or neglect towards a certain subject or issue often results into poor remembrance and hence, weaker recalling.
- Non-willingness to remember something.
- Studying and understanding a subject matter with little interest, lack of proper focus and without complete concentration.
- Continuous worries, tensions and stress also take a great toll on the ability of the mind to properly remember things.
- Peer pressure as well as continuous pressure by parents to excel in exams and competitions also burden and worry children un-

necessarily about the outcome of their exams and their future.

☞ Children are innocent and soft-hearted. Already under immense pressure in higher classes and preparation days, any uneventful mis-happening or demise of a family member is a big jolt for them.

☞ Prolonged illness or getting hurt in an accident also results into lack of proper concentration in preparations as well as during exams.

☞ Disturbed atmosphere of the family also adversely affects the concentration and understanding of children.

☞ Hereditary factors also influence children towards pursuing certain interests. If such interests are towards activities other than studies, then they are likely to have little interest in studies and hence, weaker remembrance.

In a nutshell, lack of interest and concentration in studies or certain subjects is likely to result into low understanding, low remembrance and hence, weaker retrieval of information.

Avoid Forgetting

Sometimes some children are found to be repenting about their weak memory power, inability to learn thoroughly and often forgetting their lessons. It is much found to see during the preparation and exam days. Here are some tips for better learning and good memory which put some students ahead of others. These are:

☞ It is utmost important that how these few days are spent. It makes a lot of difference in learning and scoring well. If you have been good throughout the year but got nervous or carefree during these days then all your efforts are going to get wasted. So, be cautious and alert in your approach towards your preparations.

☞ Do not overexert yourself or put extra load on your mind. Every person has his own unique set of mental capacities of working, learning and remembering. The actual problem begins when we start comparing and competing ourselves with others.

- Take frequent breaks in between studies. Try to relax your brain. Give it what it wants. It will help you save a lot of your quality time and efforts.

- Such breaks should not exceed for more than 10-15 minutes maximum. It could include a short nap with eyes closed and lying down straight; or enjoying some form of music or songs of choice; walking on fresh, clean and green grass; a quick bath or washing face, hands and feet a number of times; drinking plain water as much as possible to keep the body hydrated and for better working of the nervous system, thus keeping mental fatigue away, etc.

- But such breaks should not include watching TV or useless internet surfing; roaming or unnecessary chatting with friends; munching spicy or oily food, snacks or fast food; overeating in any way to check mood swings; or any such activity which keeps you away from your books for a longer duration.

- It is a myth that beverages like tea, coffee and cold drinks, etc. help to keep the mind fresh and alert for a longer duration. Although it gives a push to the nervous system but it is for a few minutes only. Instead, it dehydrates the body which causes more harm than good. Many a time, these drinks also cause heartburn, acidity, mouth sores and stomach ulcers for some. So, it should be avoided or used limitedly.

- Intake of tobacco products, cigarette smoking and consuming alcohol is a big 'NO', particularly during the school and college going days. This time is very crucial for the optimum development of the mind and body alike. These products can severely damage the proper growth and functioning of the mind.

- Try keeping your haircut as short as possible, especially for men. The shorter the better. It is good in keeping the mind fresh and calm naturally. At this time, it is more important to concentrate on studies, score well and be appreciated for your hard work and sincerity. In ancient India, students were kept bald head with only a small nape at the upper back of their heads during their sudent period.

- Once, the momentum of studies picks up, the understanding and learning of respective subjects begins getting better which results into good remembrance also, and gradually, self-confidence also starts building up. It further induces courage and motivation to work harder, score well and be meritorious.

📽 Do not worry much about the results, the outcome or about the future but just concentrate more on studying at the moment. Take one subject at a time. Plan your time-table yourself and divide it appropriately among different subjects, projects and other activities.

Improve Learning & Reduce Forgetting

The following suggestions will guide you to improve your learning capacities and simultaneously minimise the factors responsible for forgetting things that have relevance for us. These are:

📽 Interest and Eagerness to Learn

This is a natural phenomenon that the mind grasps and learns faster with more accuracy when the person is eager to learn something. The mental energies work in such a way that the mind retains the things better when there is an eagerness to learn.

📽 Concentration

At many times, our mind becomes a great wanderer besides being lazy at the time of putting efforts and hard work into any work. So in such situations, the mind has to be controlled effectively, motivated and its energies directed towards the work only. For this to happen, a concentrated effort is required to bear the desired results.

📽 Pictorials and Examples

Our mind learns those things faster which are presented to it by way of pictures, diagrams, video clips or by citing some examples or other interesting quotations. Students in the primary classes are taught in this way because their learning has just started.

But when there are no such things provided along with your study material, try to create your own by using your imagination. Such things take far lesser time in understanding and the time of recalling things also gets reduced. People are also able to remember such things for longer durations.

For example, a mouse is being chased by a cat, the cat is being chased by a dog and the dog is being chased by a man with a stick. By imagination, if we try to visualise the scenario then it would become quite easy for us to remember the story, and we would be able to relate and recall it easily at a future date.

☞ Relating and Logical Thinking

It becomes much easier for the mind to remember things when the newer things get related with the older things learnt earlier. Such kind of connections appears when the mind is able to form logical bonding between the new and the older data. In this way also, the mind is able to remember things for longer durations with better accuracy and faster recalling.

When you start understanding the logic of any subject matter, it becomes easier to remember it also. Similarly, when you also begin understanding the interconnections of various subjects of your syllabus as well as various issues of your life, the remembering process gets logical and easier. Hence, always try to make a connection.

☞ Attraction towards the Unusual

Our mind gets greatly attracted towards something happening in an unusual way and also all the new things that it comes across. Some examples are – a new discovery or invention; a new design or experiment; an old song being sung in a new and different way; a person using his left hand for playing a difficult game, eating and for other activities; a woman driving a heavy commercial vehicle; a person riding a bicycle with his face backwards or with folding hands, and so on. Such things remain in the mind for longer durations.

☞ Synonyms and Antonyms

Words having similar meanings are known as *synonyms,* whereas words having opposite meanings are known as *antonyms*. This is also an easy way to memorise things.

Examples of a few synonyms are: happy-joyful, sad-worried, climb-ascend, decline-descend, getting-receiving, giving-parting, and so on.

Examples of a few antonyms are: hot-cold, winter-summer, in-out, high-low, rich-poor, good-bad, happy-sad, hard working-lazy, and so on.

☞ Short Intervals and Rest

Always ensure for your mind adequate rest and relaxation by way of frequent intervals in between. This greatly enhances remembrance and storing of things that have been studied and learnt up to such breaks. Such intervals give due rest to the mind which in turn increases its capacity manifold for further learning and remembering.

☞ Music

Playing some light music along with your studies or while working helps to keep the mind relaxed as well as focused on the task at hand. It also helps to cut out on any other kind of disturbances caused by noises in the vicinity. You may choose the music of your liking so that it helps you to maintain your concentration. You may, also try playing a musical instrument in your free time to de-stress yourself.

☞ Sub-division of Bigger Topics

Though it is better to study and finish a topic in a single sitting but in case of bigger lessons it is advisable to divide such topics into two or more sections or sittings. For this, first a general reading should be carried out and thereafter such topics should be divided as per their relevance and applicability. In this way the topics are learnt more effectively while maintaining the connectivity with the main topic as well.

☞ Repetition and Practice

This is the most common and the most effective method known and followed worldwide. Learning, remembering and its retention becomes much easier and better when something is repeated. The more it is practised, the better it gets with every repetition.

Repetition of a subject matter becomes utmost important when we wish to retain the information in the same way we intend it to use it later. And, every repetition takes lesser efforts and lesser time to repeat the said subject matter and its learning. Our mind functions better in this way.

Repetition may be done either by reading, writing, listening or by practising if it is of practical nature. In all the four methods, the verbal repetition done along with can be carried out slowly in the mind or in high tone. It is adviced to be done in a higher volume, because that way the remembrance and its retention increases manifold.

For example, students of the primary school are often found to be repeating their texts in high tone. This is the best method especially for those who have just begun their education. It is also very much suitable for children who are slow learners or for those who are not able to concentrate well in their studies. Also, very effective during the examination time when the pressure is high and the time is limited to cover the study material.

Here is a very common example of the visible effects of repetition. You must have come across several tracks used by people as a shortcut from the main road. Such tracks get formed automatically later on in due course of time when used repeatedly. Similarly, a hollow is formed on the ground or even a hard stone where water falls continuously in the form of droplets or as a regular flow. Hence, repetition is always good for learning and good remembering.

☞ Inspiration and Motivation
When a person is inspired or gets motivated to do something, then the subconscious mind becomes active and takes due interest in the activities. This further enables faster learning, better remembrance and good retention as well as faster recalling in the future.

Advice: Read this chapter at least three to four times during the day today. It will help you to differentiate the different forms of the learning and remembering systems undertaken by the mind.

✳✳✳

Improve Your Memory Part - I

Today, we will test your memory by undertaking a small test. This test has been sub-divided into smaller and different parts. Though the previous chapters would have certainly given you a fair idea about the way your mind works, after taking the following tests, you will come to know the actual working capacity of your mind. This will further help you to get better in your daily approach.

Exercise 1: Some words are mentioned below. You have to read slowly and observe these words, understand them and relate them in your mind. After finishing, close the book and write them on a piece of paper. Do not forget to mention today's date before you start writing.

Banana, Moon, Bear, Mouse, Galaxy, Biscuits, Butterfly, Chair, Internet, Pen, Cow, Giraffe, Tomato, Pencil, Planets, Chalk, Rabbit, Potato, Spaceship, Astronaut, Zebra, Salt, Peacock, Rocket, Emails, Tiger, Notebook, Sugar, Jupiter, Almonds, Earth, Strawberry, Burger, Mobile Aeroplane, French, Fries, Ticket, Laptop.

(**Tip:** Rearrange all the above words in different columns as per their similarities.)

S.No.	I	II	III	IV
1.	Apple	Fish	Stars	Table
2.	Banana	Bear	Galaxy	Chair
3.	Tomato	Giraffe	Planets	Chalk
4.	Potato	Zebra	Moon	Pencil
5.	Strawberry	Rabbit	Spaceship	Notebook
6.	Biscuits	Mouse	Astronaut	Pen
7.	Sugar	Butterfly	Rocket	Laptop
8.	Salt	Peacock	Aeroplane	Internet
9.	French Fries	Tiger	Jupiter	Mobile
10.	Burger	Cow	Earth	E-mails
11.	Almonds		Ticket	

Exercise 2: Below are mentioned some birthday dates of important and lovely people in my life. Good people will always keep on getting added to this list. I will suggest you some easy ways to remember them. Accordingly, you have to prepare your own list. Kindly follow the tips. It helps to maintain good relationships with people.

Mr. Varinder Aggarwal	24 January 19	Mr. Vimal Jaitly	9 January 1974
Mr. Arun Sagar	20 November 1968	Mr. Piyush Aggarwal	6 February 1977
Mr. Vishal Mani	15 April 1975	Mr. Harinder Singh	24 January 1954
Dr. P.K. Gupta	22 October 1956	Mrs. Mamo Devi	2 January 19
Baby Ananya Singhal	2 August 2011	Mr. Aditya Gupta	2 February 1989
Miss Vibhu Aggarwal	9 March 1995	Mrs. Madhubala Nagar	9 February 19
Mr. Sanjay Singhal	5 January 1973	Mr. Sunil Madan	7 March 1961
Mr. Ashish Goel	2 February 1982	Mr. Raman Nagpal	1 March 1975
Mr. Raman Dua	25 September 1979	Miss Nikita Gupta	21 October 19
Mrs. Ranjana Aggarwal	18 April 19	Mr. Satpal Singh Bhatia	25 May 1961
Mr. Gautam Singhal	12 March 1981	Mr. Sanjay Verma	1 July 1971
Baby Diksha Bajaj	5 May 2005	Mr. Sunil Wadhwa	18 December 19

Mr.Avnish Gupta	1 May 1987	Mr.Abhishek Saxena	5 July 1980
Mr.Ranjeet Singh Bisht	14 June 1980	Mr.Naresh Kumar Bajaj	25 May 1979
Mr.Satish Kumar Aggarwal	25 June 1974	Mrs.Neha Chandel	27 July 19
Mr.Vikas Gupta	8 July 1985	Mr.Ayush Aggarwal	3 August 1996
Mr.Sanjay Dhama	1 July 1973	Mr.Karan Chawla	12 August 1984
Mr.Manjeet Singh Bisht	30 August 1978	Mr.Anil Kumar Mahajan	25 October 1965
Mr.Umesh Sharma	20 December 1956	Mr.Lalit Saini	22 September 1981
Mr.Kamal Kant Kalra	4 December 1979	Dr.Himanshi Verma	21 December 19
Mr.Chandan Pawar	23 September 1975	Mr.Gaurav Chawla	31 October 1979
Mr.Girish Bhandari	26 August 19	Dr.Kamal Kumar Kapoor	2 December 1974
Mr.Sanjeev Kumar	27 December 19	Mr.Amit Girdhar	15 January 1975
Mr.Amit Saxena	31 December 1983	Mr.Vikram Sharma	27 December 1975
Mr.Rajinder S Ahluwalia	26 August 1966	Mr.Suresh Kumar Garg	15 March 1957
Mr.Nitin Gupta	1 December 19	Mr.Prashant Kapoor	6 November 1995
Mr.Amit Puri	1 April 1978	Anil Kumar	14 April 1975

Tip 1: Make a month-wise list of the above data for better remembrance and faster recalling. Write it in ascending order.

Tip 2: Birthdays can also be easily remembered when the dates, months and years are similar with your own date of birth, e.g. all people whose date starts with 24 or falls in January, like mine. There is some matching by way of thinking or similar wavelength, -- birth numbers are divisible by: (3) 3,6,9,12,... (4) 4,8,12,... (6) 6,12,18,24,...etc. -- total or basic numbers are the same, e.g. (1,10,19-1+9=10=1+0=1,28) (3,12,21,30), (4,13,22,31), (5,14,23), (8,17,24), ... and so on.

Tip 3: The best proven way is to greet them on their special days every year. It could be by emails, message, by calling, by sending a card by post or an e-card, or presenting them a bouquet of flowers, a gift, chocolates or sweets, etc. Your relationship will get special with each passing year...

JANUARY		FEBRUARY	
Mrs.Mamo Devi	2 January 19	Mr.Aditya Gupta	2 February 1989
Mr.Sanjay Singhal	5 January 1973	Mr.Ashish Goel	2 February 1982
Mr.Vimal Jaitly	9 January 1974	Mr.Piyush Aggarwal	6 February 1977
Mr.Amit Girdhar	15 January 1975	Mrs.Madhubala Nagar	9 February 19
Mr.Varinder Aggarwal	24 January 19		
Mr.Harinder Singh	24 January 1954		
Mr.Pushpesh Dhingra	24 January 1973		

MARCH		APRIL	
Mr.Raman Nagpal	1 March 1975	Mr.Amit Puri	1 April 1978
Mr.Sunil Madan	7 March 1961	Anil Kumar	14 April 1975
Miss Vibhu Aggarwal	9 March 1995	Mr.Vishal Mani	15 April 1975
Mr.Gautam Singhal	12 March 1981	Mrs.Ranjana Aggarwal	18 April 19
Mr.Suresh Kumar Garg	15 March 1957		

MAY		JUNE	
Mr.Avnish Gupta	1 May 1987	Mr.Ranjeet Singh Bisht	14 June 1980
Baby Diksha Bajaj	5 May 2005	Mr.Satish Kumar Aggarwal	25 June 1974
Mr.Satpal Singh Bhatia	25 May 1961		
Mr.Naresh Kumar Bajaj	25 May 1979		

JULY		AUGUST	
Mr.Sanjay Verma	1 July 1971	Baby Ananya Singhal	2 August 2011
Mr.Sanjay Dhama	1 July 1973	Mr.Ayush Aggarwal	3 August 1996
Mr.Abhishek Saxena	5 July 1980	Mr.Karan Chawla	12 August 1984
Mrs.Neha Chandel	27 July 19	Mr.Rajinder S Ahluwalia	26 August 1966
Mr.Vikas Gupta	8 July 1985	Mr.Girish Bhandari	26 August 19
		Mr.Manjeet Singh Bisht	30 August 1978

SEPTEMBER		OCTOBER	
Mr.Lalit Saini	22 September 1981	Miss Nikita Gupta	21 October 19
Mr.Chandan Pawar	23 September 1975	Dr.P.K.Gupta	22 October 1956
Mr.Raman Dua	25 September 1979	Mr.Anil Kumar Mahajan	25 October 1965
		Mr.Gaurav Chawla	31 October 1979

NOVEMBER		DECEMBER	
Mr.Prashant Kapoor	6 November 1995	Mr.Nitin Gupta	1 December 19
Mr.Arun Sagar	20 November1968	Dr.Kamal Kumar Kapoor	2 December 1974

Mr.Rajeev Goyal	26 November 1984	Mr.Kamal Kant Kalra	4 December 1979
		Mr.Sunil Wadhwa	18 December 19
		Mr.Umesh Sharma	20 December 1956
		Dr.Himanshi Verma	21 December 1973
		Mr.Sanjeev Kumar	27 December 19
		Mr.Vikram Sharma	27 December 1975
		Mr.Amit Saxena	31 December 1983

✳✳✳

Improve Your Memory Part - II

Formation of Different Words

Using the letters mentioned below, create as many words as possible. You have to use all the different letters only once to form the words. So, get started.

Exercise 1: U A B T I R T S E

BETTER	BET	BEST	BITTER	BUTTER	BAT
BED	BELT	TEST	TESTER	TESTED	TREAT
SET	SETTLE	SEAT	…	…	…

Exercise 2: C E H T S R A

CARE	RACE	EAR	ACE	ARE	CAR
CASH	ASH	HAS	HAT	RAT	CAT
TEAR	SEAT	TEACH	…	…	…

Exercise 3: O T G A E S

GOAT	GATE	TAG	STAGE	STAG	SAGE
GET	ATE	GOT	OATS	…	…

Example 4: Find different eatables among the following bunch of words and encircle or highlight them. These are written as – straight forward, straight down or straight diagonally down. You may note them separately as well.

Today's Date: __ / __ / ____
(Kindly write with a Pencil)

A	P	B	E	T	C	V	X	Z	B	F	I	T	O	P	O	S	A	A	L
C	A	T	F	I	S	H	K	U	P	T	Y	O	G	U	R	T	Y	R	I
Y	N	W	B	C	U	I	P	M	L	I	C	A	S	V	Z	W	O	U	N
N	C	Y	B	A	N	A	N	A	R	O	B	S	P	I	N	A	C	H	O
Q	A	X	U	R	P	S	P	A	G	H	E	T	T	I	I	F	T	A	P
A	K	E	R	V	B	J	L	P	O	I	R	R	U	S	P	E	R	M	S
V	E	G	G	S	M	I	J	N	L	C	T	P	N	M	S	R	I	B	E
E	S	I	E	B	P	E	A	C	H	E	S	O	T	E	P	S	U	U	K
A	S	N	R	P	A	I	R	A	G	U	T	S	R	I	O	F	L	R	E
P	L	G	U	T	O	N	Z	E	P	T	R	U	I	N	T	E	A	G	L
E	V	E	U	L	T	U	R	Z	E	R	A	N	C	G	A	T	I	E	B
Y	E	R	E	L	L	O	W	P	A	U	W	H	E	A	T	R	P	R	E
L	A	M	U	F	F	I	N	S	B	L	B	E	A	R	O	L	Y	B	I
R	D	E	N	W	I	N	E	J	O	O	E	Y	T	H	E	D	A	Y	W
I	T	H	M	E	S	O	K	A	Y	B	R	E	W	I	L	M	E	A	G
A	I	N	O	C	H	I	P	S	F	O	R	A	A	L	M	O	N	D	S
X	H	E	N	H	B	L	E	A	C	H	Y	Y	N	E	W	F	O	L	D
G	A	R	L	I	C	R	A	N	E	A	G	L	E	G	D	Y	O	W	L
A	R	E	B	C	D	U	R	E	S	T	O	F	B	R	E	A	D	E	O
U	W	T	H	K	A	M	S	N	P	C	H	E	E	S	E	G	L	I	V
G	R	A	P	E	S	I	N	G	K	I	U	B	E	H	O	N	E	Y	L
E	W	A	L	N	U	T	S	A	L	T	T	V	F	E	A	S	S	T	Y

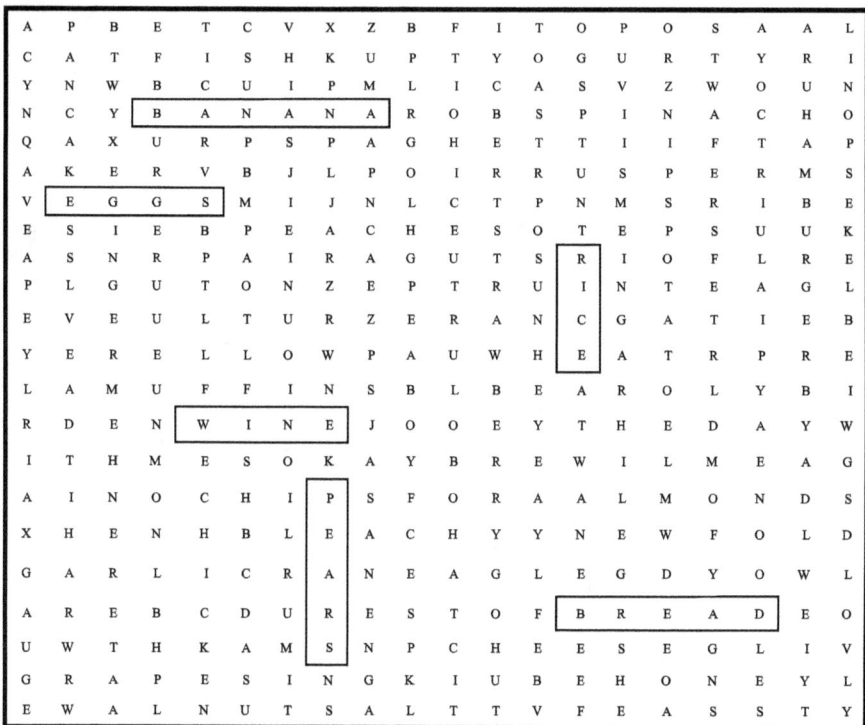

Some of them are:

Bread, Eggs, Banana, Pears, Beef, Pizza, Apple, and so on…

....
....

....
....

(Kindly use a soft pencil)

***

Code Language

Code language is a method of remembering things in an easier and comfortable way. 'Code' here means to remember things by some other name or sign. Many people use this method to remember and differentiate between different things. It could differ from person to person. Each and every person has his/her own way of thinking. You may refer other person's code, but it is better to develop your own. Let us see this through an example.

Example 1: Following is a code language for numbers that are written in words. It is just an example to make you understand. You may create your own. The idea is to remember the numbers in a simpler way by relating them with something else. You will observe a kind of tuning or rhythm in the numbers and their codes.

Numbers	Numbers in Words	Codes for Numbers
1	ONE	RUN
2	TWO	WHO
3	THREE	TREE
4	FOUR	FLOOR
5	FIVE	HIVE
6	SIX	FIX
7	SEVEN	HEAVEN
8	EIGHT	WEIGHT
9	NINE	MINE
10	TEN	DEN
11	ELEVEN	EVEN
12	TWELVE	SHELVE
13	THIRTEEN	HURTING

Today's Date: __ / __ / ____
(Kindly write with a Pencil)

14	FOURTEEN	FLOORING
15	FIFTEEN	LIFTING
16	SIXTEEN	SEEING
17	SEVENTEEN	EVENING
18	EIGHTEEN	EIGHT LANE (ROAD)
19	NINETEEN	NINTH INN
20	TWENTY	HEFTY

Exercise 1: Now let us practise the above code language. Match the words and numbers with their respective codes by drawing lines.

Numbers		Codes for Numbers
TWO		HIVE
3		HEAVEN
FIVE		SEEING
SIX		LIFTING
7		EVEN
EIGHT		TREE
10		DEN
11		WHO
TWELVE		SHELVE
FIFTEEN		WEIGHT
16		NINTH INN
NINETEEN		FIX

Example 2: Another way of coding numbers.

Z=0, A=1, B=2, C=3, D=4, E=5, F=6, G=7, H=8, I=9.

Numbers	Codes	Numbers	Codes	Numbers	Codes
21	BA	36	CF	51	EA
22	BB	37	CG	52	EB
23	BC	38	CH	53	EC
24	BD	39	CI	54	ED

25	BE	40	DZ	55	EE
26	BF	41	DA	56	EF
27	BG	42	DB	57	EG
28	BH	43	DC	58	EH
29	BI	44	DD	59	EI
30	CZ	45	DE	60	FZ
31	CA	46	DF	61	FA
32	CB	47	DG	62	FB
33	CC	48	DH	63	FC
34	CD	49	DI	64	FD
35	CE	50	EZ	65	FE

You can further relate these codes as initials in the following ways:

BA = British Airways   BF = Boy Friend   CG = College Girl

CA = Chartered Accountant   CD = CD Player   FD = Fixed Deposit

BE = Bachelor of Electronics DA = Delhi Airport   EZ = Easy

CH = Holiday in Canada   FA = First Attempt   … and so on.

Example 3: Relate the things of your shopping list with something. The more logical the connection, the better remembrance you can have.

SHOPPING LIST	CODE	REMINDED BY
MIRROR	My Beautiful Hair (as seen every morning)	Reflection in a Car Mirror
DETERGENT	Feeling of Freshness	Shining White Shirt of a Passerby
TOOTHBRUSH	My Shining Teeth	Dirty Teeth of the Shopkeeper
TEA	My Favourite Aroma Every Morning	Grocery Shop Owner Sipping Tea

CHOCOLATE	Tasty My Favourite Sweet	A Child Eating Chocolate on the Way
SHARPENER	Sharp Pencil Tip	Broken Tip of My Pencil in the Geometry Box
MEDICINE	Lifeline of My Grandfather	An Elderly Coughing Nearby
MOBILE BATTERY CHARGER	I Cannot do without My Mobile	Low Battery Beep by the Mobile Handset

✱✱✱

SELF-IMPROVEMENT/PERSONALITY DEVELOPMENT

Also Available
in Hindi

Also Available
in Hindi

Also Available
in Kannada, Tamil

Also Available
in Kannada

Also Available
in Kannada

All books available at www.vspublishers.com

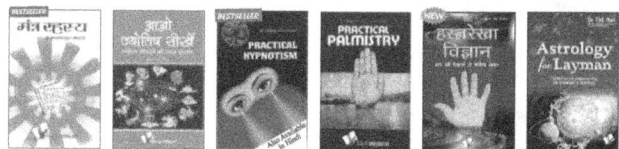

Contact us at sales@vspublishers.com

STUDENT DEVELOPMENT/LEARNING

POPULAR SCIENCE

Also Available in Hindi

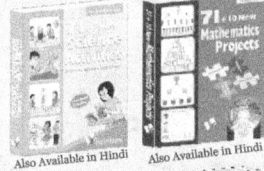

Also Available in Hindi   Also Available in Hindi

PUZZLES

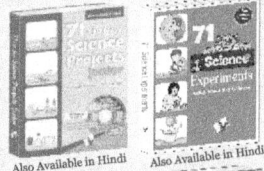

Also Available in Hindi   Also Available in Hindi

DRAWING BOOKS

Also Available in Hindi   Also Available in Hindi, Tamil & Bangla

CHILDREN'S ENCYCLOPEDIA – THE WORLD OF KNOWLEDGE

Contact us at sales@vspublishers.com